我的一生

目錄

ABOUT ME

This is me

My name is

I am   years old

I come from

I speak in

Name, age, country, language

This is what I look like

Things I like

e.g. music, sport, food, clothes, games, dancing, computers, reading books or magazines, cooking, film stars, singers, places

Things I am good at

e.g. maths, science, sport, singing, dancing, athletics

I am

(Height: tall, short, medium...)

And I have
(eyes: blue, brown, green, hazel
hair: light, dark, brown, black, blonde, fair, short, long, curly, straight, wavy)

My Friends

old friends   new friends

2

有關我自己

這是我

我的姓名是…

我的年齡是…

我來自…

我的語言是…

姓名，年齡，國籍，語言

我的模樣

我的喜好

例如：音樂，運動，食物，衣服，遊戲，
跳舞，電腦，讀書本或看雜誌，烹飪，
電影明星，歌星，名勝

我擅長的事項

例如：數學，科學，運動，
唱歌，跳舞，田徑體育

我的身材…

高度：高，矮，中等高度

而我有…

眼睛：藍色，綠色，棕色
頭髮：淺色，深色，棕色，黑色，金色，
淺色，短，長，卷曲，直，起伏式
眼睛：藍色，綠色，棕色

我的朋友

舊朋友，新朋友

MY FAMILY

Relatives

Sister, brother, cousin
Parents: mother, father
uncle, aunt, stepmother, stepfather,
Grandparents: grandmother, grandfather

Generations

My generation, my parents' generation
the older generation, the younger generation

Size of family

Number of brothers and sisters,
names and ages of brothers and sisters,
number of aunts, uncles and cousins

On the next page a family tree has been drawn for you to complete

我的家庭

姐妹，兄弟，堂（表）兄弟姐妹

父母 — 母親，父親

叔伯（舅）父，姑（姨）母，
繼母，繼父

祖父母 — 祖母（外婆），
祖父（外公），曾祖母，曾祖父

祖輩世代

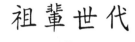

我的一代，我父母的一代
祖輩，下一代

家庭結構大小

兄弟和姐妹的數目
兄弟和姐妹的姓名和年齡
姑（姨）母，叔伯（舅）父，
堂（表）兄弟姐妹的數目

下一頁有一個家系圖供你填寫。

MY FAMILY TREE

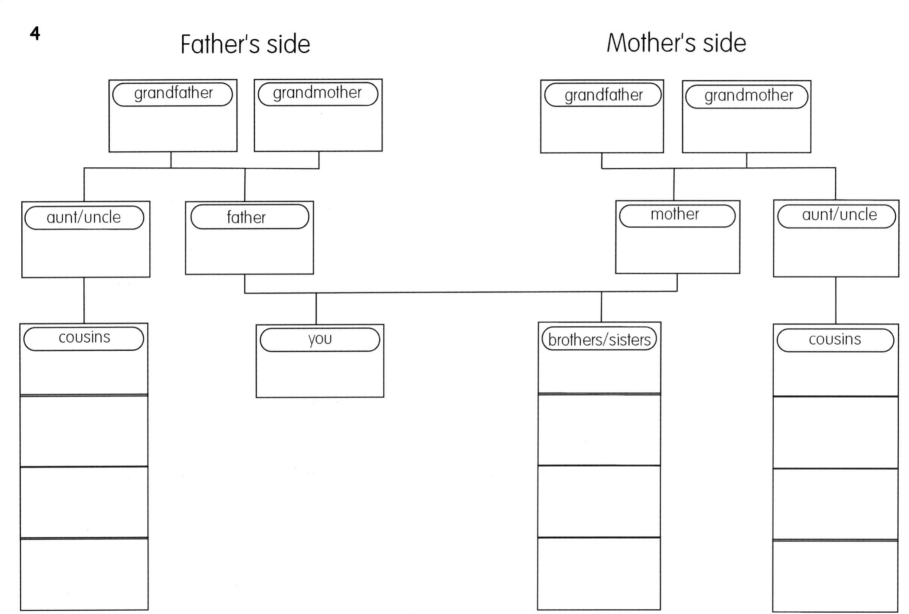

Father's side

Mother's side

grandfather	grandmother
father	aunt/uncle
cousins	you

grandfather	grandmother
mother	aunt/uncle
brothers/sisters	cousins

我的家系圖

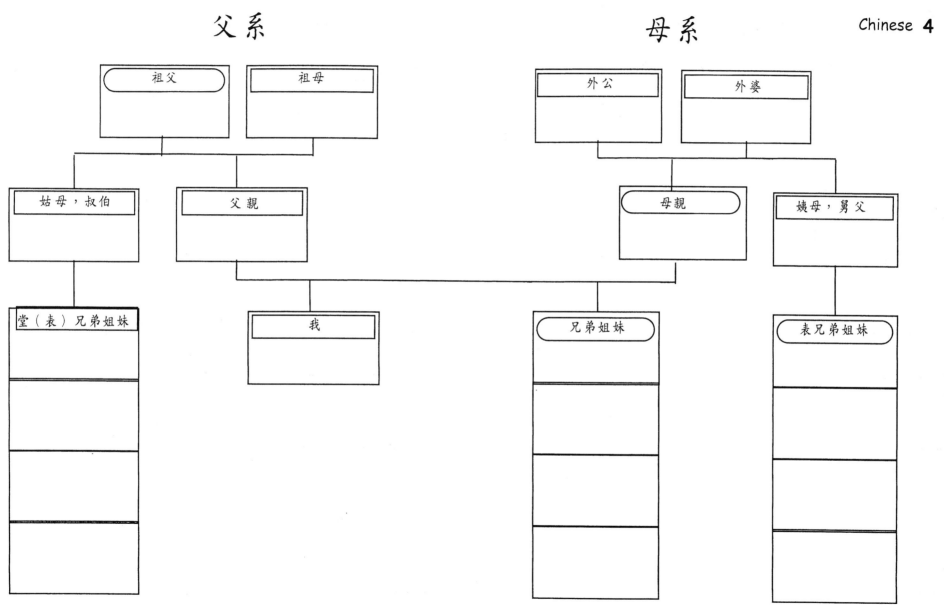

父系　　　　　　　　　　母系

祖父　　　祖母　　　　　　外公　　　外婆

姑母，叔伯　　　父親　　　　　母親　　　姨母，舅父

堂（表）兄弟姐妹　　我　　　　　兄弟姐妹　　　表兄弟姐妹

MORE ABOUT MY FAMILY

更多有關我的家庭

History of My Country

Important dates Important events

Traditions and festivals

Special clothes and food

People of My Country

Religion, languages

MY COUNTRY

Geography of My Country

Size, population, rivers, mountains,
capital city, other main cities

Food in My Country

What do farmers grow?
What food do people eat at festivals?
Types of food: Fish, meat, vegetables,
fruit, cereals, dairy products

Famous People from My Country

Leaders, musicians, singers, artists,
scientists, filmstars, footballers

我祖國的歷史

重要的日子　　重要的大事

我祖國的傳統和節日

特別的服式和食品

我祖國的民族

宗教，語言

我的祖國

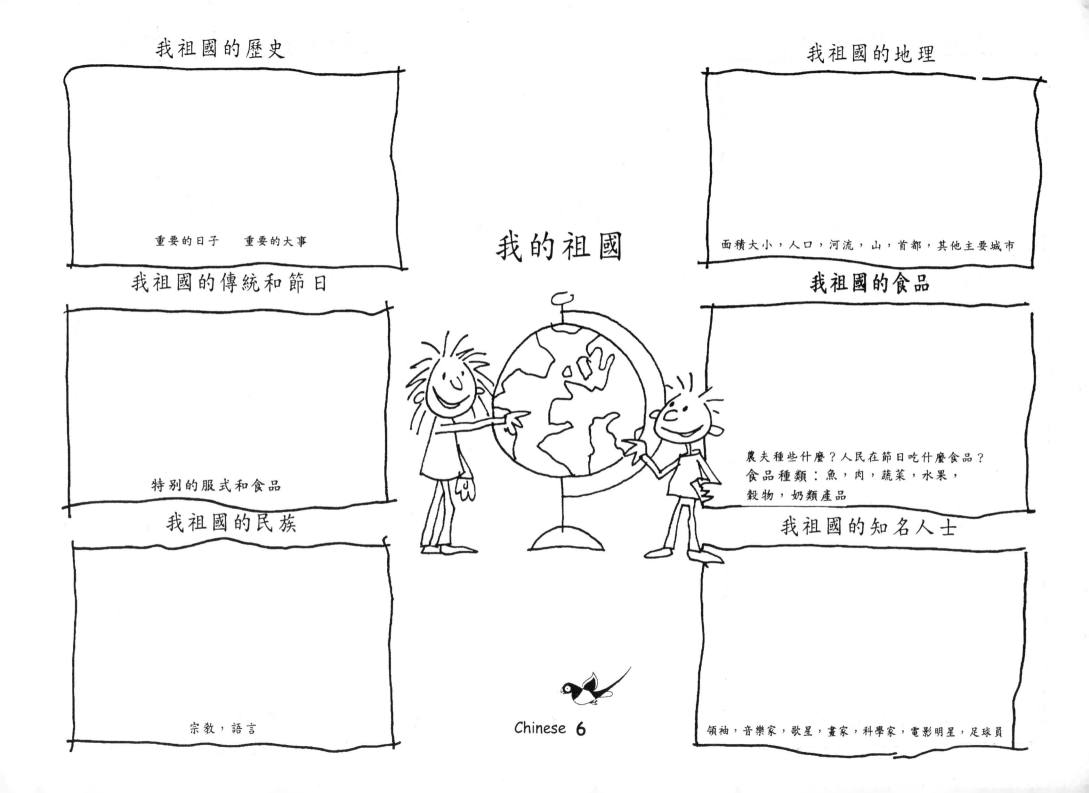

我祖國的地理

面積大小，人口，河流，山，首都，其他主要城市

我祖國的食品

農夫種些什麼？人民在節日吃什麼食品？
食品種類：魚，肉，蔬菜，水果，
穀物，奶類產品

我祖國的知名人士

領袖，音樂家，歌星，畫家，科學家，電影明星，足球員

MY MEMORIES OF CHILDHOOD

Where were you born and what are your memories of your family, your friends, your life and your first school?

I was born in.............................(place)
        in ....(year)

My family lived there for........................... years.

My earliest memory is when...

I also can remember the time when...

I first went to school in...............(country)   in................(year)

My first teachers were ...

My best friends were...

I used to like...

I used to play...

If I go back to my country now, I would like to...

兒時的回憶

你在那裏出生的？你對你的家庭，你的朋友，你的一生和你的
第一間學校記得多少？

我是在……　　　　　　（年份）

在……　　　　　　　　　　（地點）出生的。

我的家人在那裏住了……年

我最初的記憶是在………

我亦記得那次………

我第一次上學是在……（年份）

在……（國家）

我最初的老師是……

我最好的朋友是……

我以前一向喜歡……

我以前一向都玩……

如果我現在返回我的祖國，我希望……

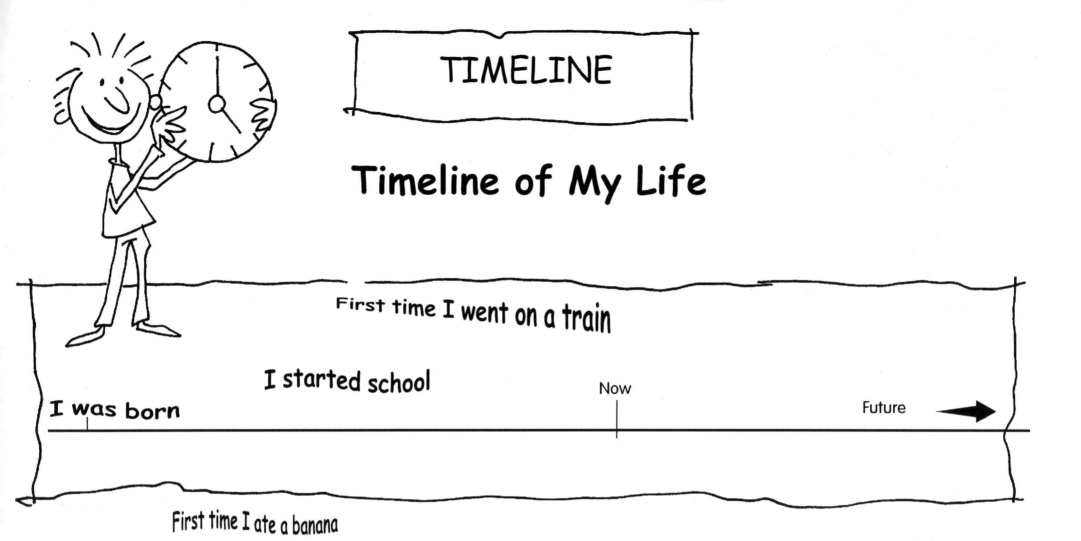

TIMELINE

Timeline of My Life

First time I went on a train

I started school

Now

I was born

Future

First time I ate a banana

Enjoyed new year

I learnt to swim

8

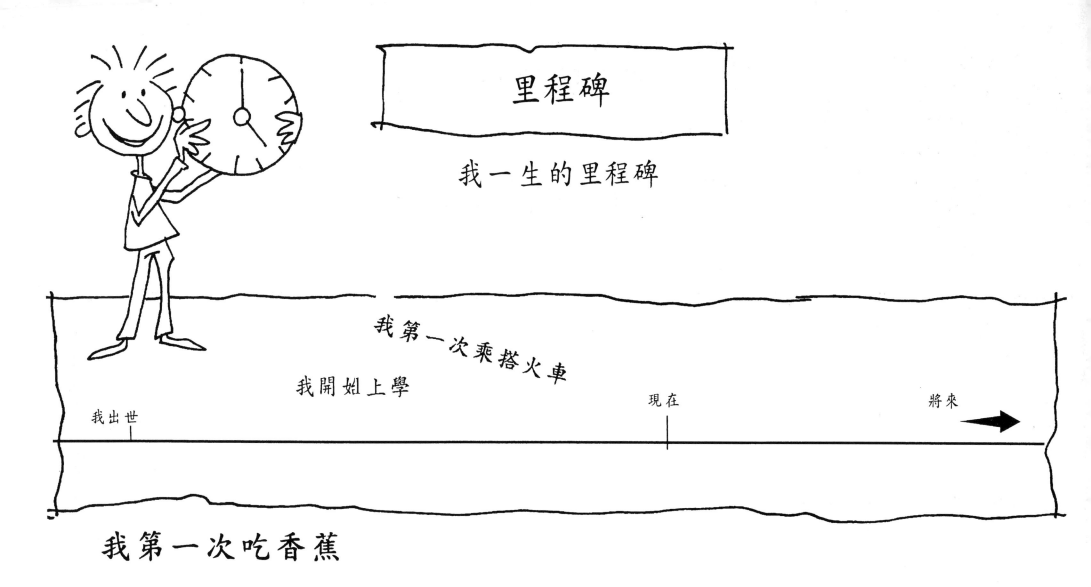

里程碑

我一生的里程碑

我第一次乘搭火車

我開始上學

我出世　　　　　　　　　　　　　　現在　　　　　　　將來

我第一次吃香蕉

新年享樂

我學游泳

ONE THING I WILL NEVER FORGET

Describe something that happened in your home country or coming to this country

I will never forget the time when...

Events
New baby in the family, birthday, family gathering, holiday, wedding, festival, war, fighting, death, torture, invasion, cease-fire, escape, shortage of water/food, running away

我永遠都不會忘記的一件事

描述一些在你的祖國或到這個國家時發生的事情。

我永遠不會忘記那次……

事件場合

家中添丁，生日，家庭聚會，假期，婚禮，節日，戰爭，爭斗，

死亡，痛苦虐待，侵襲，停火休戰，逃亡，缺糧／水，逃走。

MY SCHOOLING

(Experience of previous schools in home country)

First school, first memories, other children, teachers, best friends, best teachers

What was your first school like- what languages were used by children, parents and teachers?

I first went to school in...

Children start school at the age of...

My class teacher was...

My school was...

My best friends were...

The languages spoken were...

我的上學經歷
（以前的學校和在祖國的經歷）

第一間學校，最初的記憶，其他兒童，教師，最好的朋友，最好的老師

你第一間學校是怎樣的？說什麼語言？

我最初上學是在……

我的班主任老師是……

我最好的朋友是……

兒童開始上學的年齡是……

我的學校是……

所說的語言是……

Chinese 10

COMING TO SCHOOL HERE

(first experiences of school here)

Interview day...

First day at school...

First impressions of the school: size, rules, teachers, pupils...

First friends...

First feelings: happy, unhappy, scared, excited, lost, worried...

Things I liked most when I came to school in this country...

Things I liked least about school in this country...

到這裏上學

（在這個國家的學校的最初經歷）

接見當日…

最初的感受：開心，不快樂，恐懼，興奮，失落，憂慮

第一天上學…

到這個國家的學校上學令我最喜歡的事情…

對學校的最初感覺：規模大小，校規，教師，學生

最初的朋友

這個國家的學校令我最不喜歡的事情…

WHAT I FEEL ABOUT MY SCHOOL

(describe your school, your friends and teachers)

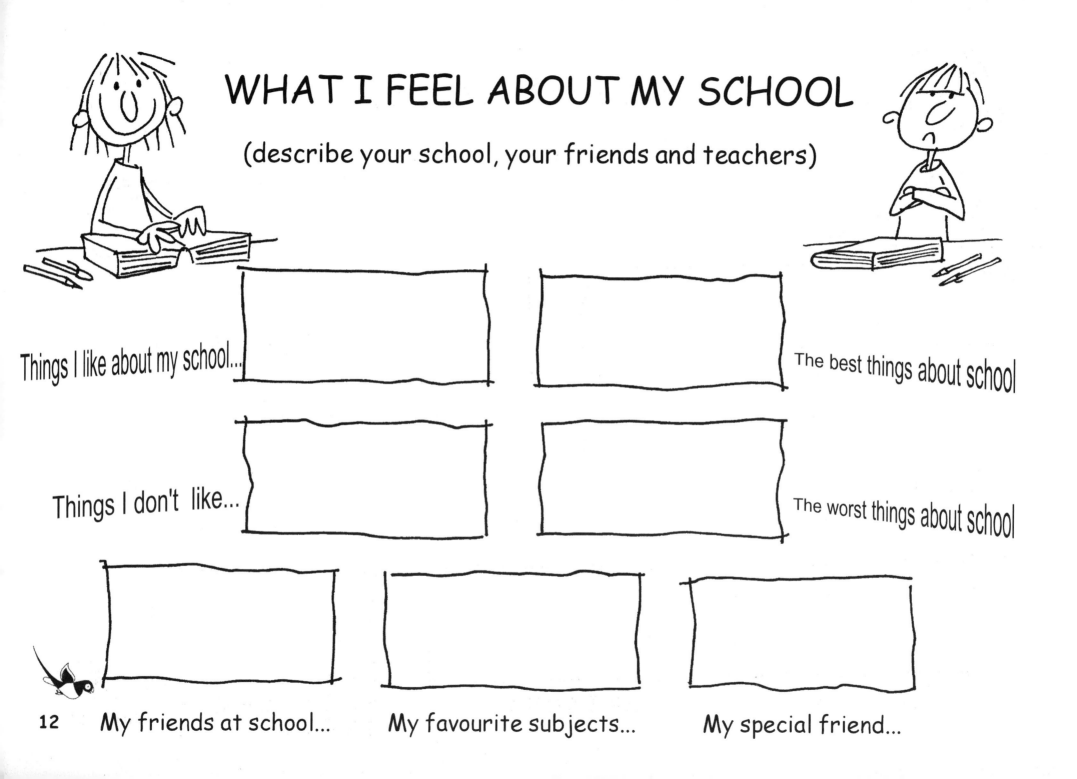

Things I like about my school...

The best things about school

Things I don't like...

The worst things about school

My friends at school...

My favourite subjects...

My special friend...

12

我對我的學校的感覺

（形容你的學校，你的朋友和老師）

我喜歡有關學校的事項

有關學校最好的事項

我不喜歡的事項

有關學校最不好的事項

我在學校的朋友…

我最喜歡的科目…

我的特別朋友—成年人，
老師或學生…

我對將來的期望

我對我的將來的期望…

我的家庭對我的期望…

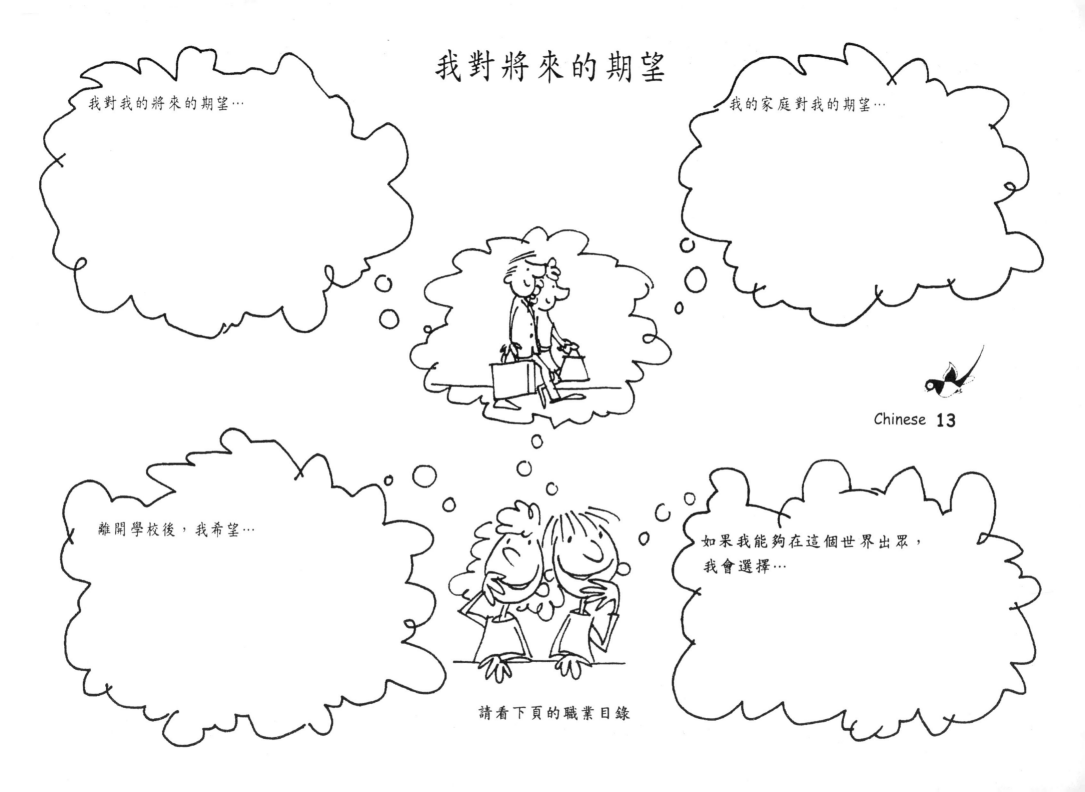

離開學校後，我希望…

請看下頁的職業目錄

如果我能夠在這個世界出眾，
我會選擇…

JOBS AND CAREERS

accountant	computer engineer	landscape gardener	police officer
actor	computer programmer	lawyer	priest
airline worker	dentist	librarian	receptionist
architect	designer	machinist	salesman
artist	disc jockey (DJ)	make-up artist	scientist
author	doctor	mechanic	secretary
banker	driving instructor	musician	shop worker
beauty therapist	editor	nurse	shopkeeper
builder	electrical engineer	nursery nurse	solicitor
bus driver	engineer	optician	stage designer
businessman/woman	farmer	park ranger	surgeon
car mechanic	film/TV producer	personal assistant	surveyor
casual worker	fire fighter	pharmacist	teacher
chef	footballer	photographer	therapist
childminder	hairdresser	pilot	train driver
civil engineer	heating engineer	plasterer	travel agent
civil servant	interpreter	playgroup assistant	veterinary surgeon (vet)
classroom assistant	journalist	playgroup organiser	zoo keeper
clerical worker	lab technician	plumber	

Jobs and Careers

accountant
actor
airline worker
architect
artist
author
banker
beauty therapist
builder
bus driver
businessman/woman
car mechanic
casual worker
chef
childminder
civil engineer
civil servant
classroom assistant
clerical worker

computer engineer
computer programmer
dentist
designer
disc jockey (DJ)
doctor
driving instructor
editor
electrical engineer
engineer
farmer
film/TV producer
fire fighter
footballer
hairdresser
heating engineer
interpreter
journalist
lab technician

landscape
gardener
lawyer
librarian
machinist
make-up artist
mechanic
musician
nurse
nursery nurse
optician
park ranger
personal
assistant
pharmacist
photographer
pilot
plasterer
play group
assistant
play group
organiser
plumber

police officer
priest
receptionist
salesman
scientist
secretary
shop worker
shopkeeper
solicitor
stage designer
surgeon
surveyor
teacher
technician
therapist
train driver
travel agent
veterinary surgeon (vet)
zoo keeper

WORDS TO DESCRIBE FEELINGS

Feelings about people

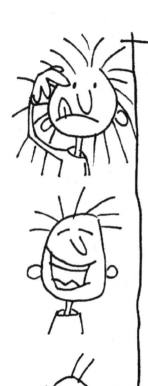

Adjectives

aggressive
anti-social
argumentative
attractive
bad
bad-tempered
beautiful
clever
cross
evil
friendly
generous
gentle
good
horrible
intelligent
kind

lively
mad
nasty
nice
popular
pretty
sensitive
silly
sociable
spiteful
strong
stupid
unkind
warm

Verbs

admire
care for
dislike
envy
hate
help
hug
kiss
like
protect

Nouns

admiration
anger
argument
beauty
envy
friendliness
gentleness
hatred
intelligence
kindness
liveliness
love
meanness
popularity
respect
sensitivity
spite
strength
stupidity
warmth

形容感受的字句

對人的感受

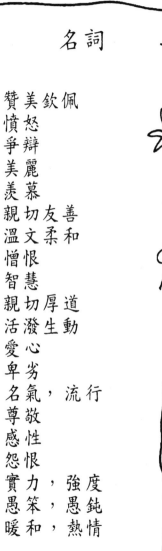

形容詞

侵略性的
厭惡的
好爭辯的
有吸引力的
差劣的
暴躁的
美麗的
互相沖突的
邪惡的
友善的
寬大的
溫文的
討厭的
仁慈的
社交的
惡毒的
慷慨的
聰明的
善良的
文智的

活潑的
瘋狂的
惡劣的
美好的
受歡迎的
漂亮的
討厭的
敏捷的
無聊的
深靈的
無際的
固執的
愚蠢的
強壯的
怨恨的
溫和的
善良的
不溫暖的

動詞

拜
崇
掛念
賞心
喜歡
欣賞
關心
不美
羨慕
厭惡
憎
幫助
擁抱
吻
喜照
愛料
保護

名詞

欽佩
美麗
憤怒
爭辯
羨慕
親切
文
智慧
厚心
發劣
道氣
敬性
溫恨
親智
活力
愛卑
名尊
感怨
實愚
溫暖

善良
和
友誼
柔
厚道
流行
強度
熱情
鈍
感
暖

WORDS TO DESCRIBE FEELINGS

Feelings about events

I was

afraid
angry
annoyed
anxious
disappointed
excited
happy
hurt
pleased
sad
surprised
terrified
worried

It was

awful
dangerous
disappointing
exciting
frightening
interesting
lovely
terrible
terrifying
violent
wonderful

Verbs

enjoy
expect
feel
fear
hope
want
worry

Nouns

anxiety
danger
disappointment
excitement
fear
happiness
pain
pleasure
terror
violence

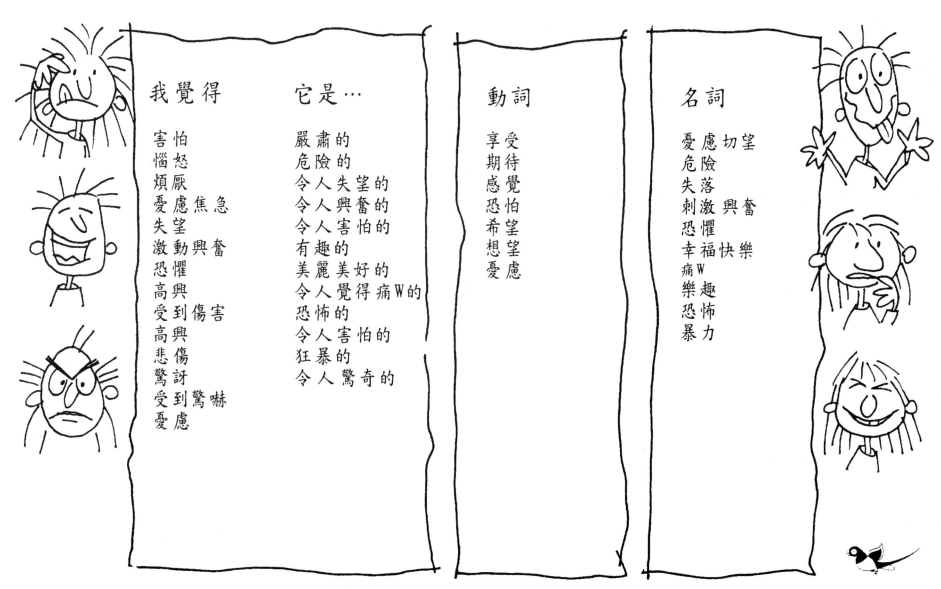

形容感受的字句
對事件場合的感受

我覺得 | **它是…** | **動詞** | **名詞**

Teachers' Notes

This book has been designed for the use of all children, but especially with bilingual children in mind.
It can be used as a whole pack or in individual parts. There is therefore no specific order.
It could be beneficial for children to share the book with their parents or carers.
Bilingual children should be encouraged to write in their first language as well as in English.

Mantra
5 Alexandra Grove, London N12 8NU
www.mantrapublishing.com